The Fox and the Grapes

by Jennifer Zimmer
illustrated by Scott Nickel

Decodable 28

Big Grapes 3
Her Grapes 5
Bad Grapes 8

McGraw Hill Education

Bothell, WA • Chicago, IL • Columbus, OH • New York, NY

MHEonline.com

Send all inquiries to:
McGraw-Hill Education
8787 Orion Place
Columbus, OH 43240

ISBN: 978-0-02-143360-5
MHID: 0-02-143360-7

Printed in China

9 10 11 12 13 DSS 28 27 26 25 24

Big Grapes

Fox sees big grapes up there.

Fox likes grapes.

Fox yips, "If I can get grapes, we can fix jam. Yum!"

Her Grapes

Fox has a plan.

She can just jump up there.

Fox sees her grapes and jumps.
But she cannot get her grapes.

Fox zigzags and hops.
Fox yelps.
Fox cannot get the grapes!

Bad Grapes

Fox has no grapes.
"We cannot fix jam," yips Fox.
"The grapes must be bad!"